# Building Lifetime Loyal Relationships

**45 Golden Nuggets
for Business Success**

By

# Alice Hinckley and Melynda Lilly

©2017 by Alice Hinckley and Melynda Lilly

All rights reserved. Except as permitted as under the U.S. Copyright Act of 1976, no part of this publication may be reproduced, distributed, or transmitted in any form or by any means, or stored in a database or retrieval system, without the prior written permission of the author.

# TABLE OF CONTENTS

| | | | |
|---|---|---|---|
| 1 | Relationship with Yourself | Tips 1-8 | Pg 9 |
| 2 | Social Media Relationships | Tips 8-17 | Pg 17 |
| 3 | Team Relationships | Tips 18-24 | Pg 26 |
| 4 | Family & Friends | Tips 25-31 | Pg 33 |
| 5 | Mentors | Tips 32-37 | Pg 40 |
| 6 | Referral Network | Tips 38-45 | Pg 46 |

Dedicated to:

Our TEAM!

Who is our team?

Everyone that is part of our lives:
Our husbands
Business partners
Family
Friends
Colleagues
Referral Networks
Vendors & Suppliers

# INTRODUCTION

People make us happy!

Life is really all about relationships. Having the savvy to build strong, lifetime relationships will not only give your life amazing texture, it will build your business on a strong foundation.

Having been friends for over twenty years, with both of us creating many other lifelong relationships, we desire to help you feel confident in your ability to connect immediately while setting the stage for a lifetime of mutual benefit.

Take each area to heart as we share tips on building a strong relationship with yourself, keeping social media relationships relevant, creating mutually beneficial relationships with your team, deepening your relationship with your family and friends, integrating relationships with your mentors, and solidifying your relationship with your referral network.

You have the potential. Embrace some of the practices that we do naturally after many years and watch the relationships in your life deepen and grow stronger.

Encourage people. Enjoy people. Meet new people. Develop stronger relationships with people you are drawn to in business and life.

People make life truly rich. Embrace them!

Relationship with Yourself
Tip 1

**Invest in Yourself**

CANI, **C**onstant **A**nd **N**ever-ending **I**mprovement, can be applied to all areas of your life. Make a decision to learn each and every day. Each book you read, seminar you attend, CD you listen to—just one idea could change your life forever. Start today investing in yourself. YOU are worth it!

"Investing in yourself is the best investment you will ever make. It will not only improve your life, it will improve the lives of all those around you."
--Robin Sharma

Relationship with Yourself
Tip 2

**Treasure Maps**

For the past twenty years, every January we have created a treasure map (now popularly known as a vision board). It is a collage of pictures & words that you want to have, be or do in your life.

Simply cutout pictures & words from magazines then paste them on a poster board. Place your vision board where you will see it daily. It keeps you focused on your goals & dreams.

Make sure to use power words on your board. "I feel healthy. I feel happy. I feel terrific." Great way to start your day!

Relationship with Yourself
Tip 3

## Goals with a Purpose

Setting specific goals is a vital key to success in your business and your life. Goals without a "why" will not compel you forward. You must have a reason to reach the goal. An excellent formula to write a compelling goal is:

On or before (date), I will _(your goal)_ because _(the reason it is important to you to achieve the goal)_.

Relationship with Yourself
Tip 4

**Healthy is Wealthy**

To enjoy all your relationships with friends, family and business associates, you must feel strong and vibrant. It is crucial to implement healthy self-care practices such as...

Getting fresh air & sunshine—take a walk.
Hydrate yourself with lots of water.
Make nutritious food choices—skip the fast food.
Nurture yourself at least monthly—get a massage.

You know how to make your body stronger. Take positive action every day towards a healthy body for real wealth.

Relationship with Yourself
Tip 5

**Work Hard, Play Hard**

You are driven to succeed and make a difference in the lives of other people. However, if you work ten or more hours 6-7 days a week, you will be drained and not operate at an optimal level. We know you work hard so be sure to play hard.

Schedule vacations with those you love.
Get on the golf course, tennis courts, softball field, go hunting-- and have some fun!
Learn to scuba dive & take a tropical trip.
Do something that stretches you like sky diving.

Reward Yourself! You Deserve It!

Relationship with Yourself
Tip 6

**JACKPOTS!**

When you achieve a goal be sure to celebrate your accomplishment!
\*\*Enjoy a meal at your favorite restaurant with family & friends. Order the chocolate cake & the champagne!\*\*
\*\*Have a full spa day with massage, facial, manicure, pedicure and more.\*\*
\*\*Take a weekend getaway to your favorite hotel or resort.\*\*
\*\*Have a celebration party for promotions, graduations, birthdays, etc.\*\*
\*\*Celebrate everything big or small!\*\*

"The more you praise and celebrate your life, the more there is in life to celebrate!"   ---Oprah Winfrey

Relationship with Yourself
Tip 7

**Self-Talk: The Never Ending Tape in Your Brain**

Your creator made your brain like a target-guided missile system. Whatever you focus on becomes a reality in your life. Time to convert doubt to certainty by changing what you say when you talk to yourself. Try using these power phrases:

Instead of "I'll try" say "I will"
Instead of "I might be able to" say "What I can commit to is"
Instead of "It's just my opinion" say "I recommend"
Instead of "I can't" say "I will"
Instead of thinking "I'm not enough" think "I am able to"

Relationship with Yourself
Tip 8

**Suit Up to Show Up!**

You only have a few seconds to make a first impression.
Dress for success.

People will evaluate you based on your appearance and how you are dressed. Make sure your clothes are clean, hair is well groomed and make-up is neat. You don't have to spend a fortune to be crisp, sharp and professionally presentable.

Remember a warm, friendly smile makes for a great first impression. Make eye contact. When you are talking, ask lots of questions about them first. Get to know the person. We all prefer to do business with people we know, like and trust.

Social Media Relationships
Tip 9

**What NOT to Say**

Social media shows your life and attitudes to the entire globe. What is recorded on social media never goes away. Since you are building a professional image with the goal of people wanting to have a business relationship with you, it is important to avoid controversial subjects.

The basic guidelines are...
No foul language.
No sexual content.
Avoid political opinions & advertisements.
Be cautious about the religious content you share.

Your online personal life will affect the results in your business. Be wise online.

Social Media Relationships
Tip 10

**Lifestyle**

People are attracted to happy, fun, positive lifestyles. Post pictures & videos of your life on social media. People love to look at pictures and watch short videos. Before social media people would buy magazines to see how the rich and famous lived. Now they have Facebook, Twitter, Instagram,
Pinterest and so much more, to view the lives of all their family and friends.

Remember, a picture is worth a thousand words. Show everyone the happiness you are experiencing. Post your vacations, holiday traditions, sporting events, accomplishments, etc. You are famous in your circle of influence. People will value your lifestyle and want to live the kind of live you have created.

Social Media Relationships
Tip 11

**Videos**

Why are people drawn to videos on social media? Communication is a three-part process: Words, Tone of Voice and Body Language. Your words represent 7% of your communication while your tone of voice is 38% & your body language is 55%. For the most effective communication, consider not just your words but the tone you use and the way you hold your body. When you post a video, you have used words, tone of voice and body language to communicate. It allows the highest level of connection with your viewer.

Choose something you enjoy in your life and make a short video about it a couple of times a week to post online.
If you love to travel, make a quick video when you arrive & when you depart on trips. Your audience will embrace your lifestyle and warmly anticipate your next video.

Social Media Relationships
Tip 12

**A Picture is Worth a Thousand Words**

It is not only important to show pictures of yourself, use other images when making posts on social media, When posting quotes or comments, find a photo online that shows visually what you are saying in the post.

For example, if you are quoting an expert, have a picture of the expert displayed with your post. If you are showing lifestyle choices such as planning a trip to Fiji, have a gorgeous picture of the Fijian islands or a spectacular sunset over the Pacific Ocean displayed with your comments.

Having visual images makes your comments stand out from the crowd on social media.

Social Media Relationships
Tip 13

**Best Face Forward**

Positive people attract other positive people. Grumpy, negative people repel others---except for other grumpy, negative people. Therefore, always put your best face forward on social media.

Most of us were raised with the saying, "If you can't say something nice, don't say anything at all."

It is important to always be upbeat & positive. If you are having a rough day, it's acceptable to say so as long as you show it as a stepping stone to improvement. For example, if you went to Starbucks to meet a potential client and they didn't show up, you might be crazy frustrated. Say so and then share how you invested the time say hello to others having a coffee and started new relationships.

Social Media Relationships
Tip 14

**Building Rapport**

Stop selling and focus on learning about others. Interact with the posts of people you want to do business with or already have a secure business relationship.

If you constantly post about your business, you are selling, selling, selling. To develop relationships, you want to be sharing, adding value, connecting at least 80% of the time.

Over and over again it has been proven that 80% of your social media content should be focused on helping others improve, adding value to their lives, and encouraging them to live the life of their dreams. Less than 20% of your content should be about your company, your business or selling the audience on your product or service.

Social Media Relationships
Tip 15

**The Spotlight: Recognizing Others**

Whether it is someone on your team, one of your suppliers or a client, recognize them on social media. What have they accomplished in their personal or professional life? Did they receive an award for community service? Did the youth baseball team they coach reach the finals? Maybe they earned a car or a trip or a promotion. Give them a standing ovation by sharing their hard work and outstanding accomplishment.

What a special way to recognize those with a true servant's heart! Normally, these people stay far outside of the spotlight. With admiration take a moment to shine the spotlight on someone who is always giving and doing for others.

"Be so busy giving recognition that you don't need it."
--Jim Rohn

Social Media Relationships
Tip 16

**GIVE, GIVE, GIVE**

Before you ask people to give to you, you must give generously to them. It is imperative to give valuable information and resources before you ask for anything from your audience. What is an important lesson you recently learned from one of your mentors? Share the guidance, how it impacted a specific interaction in your life, and how others can use the lesson to help them move forward in their business.

We have all learned lessons through difficult and challenging situations. You can be a mentor to people you don't know personally by sharing your experience, the lessons you learned and share how they can immediately improve their life by applying the principles.

Social Media Relationships
Tip 17

**The Power of Being Real**

You are an amazing person! Be authentic! Show the incredible person you have become because of your life. Share trials & lessons. Share the amazing highs and what they taught you.
Don't fake it. Today people see through making it up as you go.

Be Real!
What are you experiencing?
How can it help you achieve your goals in the long term?
What are you feeling?
Will those feelings compel you forward or paralyze you?
How can you redirect those feelings if they are stopping you?

When you honestly share your experiences, others become deeply connected to you.

T.E.A.M. Relationships
**T**ogether **E**veryone **A**chieves **M**ore
Tip 18

**Elevator Calls**

Just like an elevator lifts you up to the top of a high-rise, a quick phone call can lift the spirits of a team member. Maybe you are calling to express gratitude for hard work or an accomplishment. A quick thank you for their loyalty as a client will likely surprise them and increase their commitment to doing business with you in the future.

Making elevator calls to raise the spirits of the person you are calling is all about them. Don't sell them anything or ask for a favor. Just call to let them know you admire their character or their commitment or how they wisely handled a difficult situation. Your call may spur the recipient forward in one of their goals just because you took the time to share a word of encouragement.

T.E.A.M. Relationships
Together Everyone Achieves More
Tip 19

**Let Them Know You Care**

Building a strong relationship with your team involves knowing why they are committed to success in their business. What are they striving to achieve? How can you help them? Asking questions about why they work hard will give you insight to help motivate and encourage them in the future.

What are some reasons people work hard in business?
**Paying for children's education**Having more freedom in retirement**Giving more to your favorite charity**Paying off debt**Providing a good lifestyle for their family**Creating magic moments such a exotic family vacations**

T.E.A.M. Relationships
**T**ogether **E**veryone **A**chieves **M**ore
Tip 20

### Events

Live events build belief! If you are in the direct selling industry or building a corporate sales team, getting people to live events to learn about the company builds deeper belief in why they want to work towards their goals. Events get people connected to the company and to one another. Events create growth in your business. People enjoy being part of something bigger than themselves.

Planning special events for your team also makes them feel a part of something important. Have a barbeque or cookout. Host a cocktail party and have everyone bring an appetizer to share. Being a participant in the event by bringing an item makes people feel more a part of the team.

T.E.A.M. Relationships
**T**ogether **E**veryone **A**chieves **M**ore
Tip 21

**Personal Notes**

The art of the handwritten note is almost lost in the world today. Set aside a time once a week on your calendar to take 30 minutes and write a note to some of your team members. Keep in mind your team includes everyone in your life that helps keep your personal and professional life in good working order. Could be your insurance agent, your assistant, a business partner, your printer, your web designer or a customer.

You get the idea. You can get boxes of cards reasonably priced. Take the time to write a note of appreciation for how they provide great service to you or a note thanking them for being a loyal client. If someone sends you a referral, it is vital to send a personal note thanking them for thinking of you.

T.E.A.M. Relationships
Together Everyone Achieves More
Tip 22

**Connection Calls**

Business is all about relationships. People want to do business with those they feel connected to as more than just a sale. Block out time in your calendar twice a week for half an hour to make phone calls to people in your circle of influence.

The purpose of a connection call is to ask questions and learn more about the person. Ask about their family. Ask about what they have been doing for fun lately. If you know they play golf, ask about where they played their last round. If you know they like to travel, ask about a recent or upcoming trip. To end the call, ask if there is anything you can help them with for their business or their family. You are consciously building a long-term relationship when you truly get to know the people on your team.

T.E.A.M. Relationships
**T**ogether **E**veryone **A**chieves **M**ore
Tip 23

**TEAM Environment**

The leader sets the stage for the team! You are responsible to create a positive, energetic environment. Whether you build a positive or a negative environment will based on your attitude as the leader. If you are negative, always complaining, focusing on the worst in people or situations, you will attract negativity. If you are high energy and positive, you will create a team of happy, positive, energetic achievers. Focus on the good in people.

Even when there is failure or a tough situation, handle it and then ask everyone what they learned from the situation. You have the power to turn a negative into a positive. Take the lead and show others how to control uncomfortable or negative situations and make them a learning, growing experience.

T.E.A.M. Relationships
**T**ogether **E**veryone **A**chieves **M**ore
Tip 24

**Be Available**

Commit to being available to your team via phone, email, text and in person. It is vital the people on your team know you are committed to their success. If you own a business, your employees need to know you are there for them to support their personal goals and will celebrate their achievements.

In business, you must respond when they have questions or concerns or need guidance to complete tasks. Being available lets them know you value the work they are doing for your business and you value them as a person. Because they recognize your commitment to your business as well as your employees, they will work harder to help the business reach milestones. Commit to yourself to be available and stay true to that commitment.

Family & Friends
Tip 25

## Vacations

Want to know the secret to happy, healthy relationships with your family and friends? Vacations! Vacations! Vacations!

It is so important to take vacations with family and friends. You don't have to spend a fortune to create lifetime memories. For years our family vacations were camping trips. We included friends. Our campouts grew to 70 people! We have moved from tents to cabins but we still take an annual family & friend's trip to Broken Bow in Oklahoma.

Taking a vacation with just your spouse is also important—especially if you have children. You need time alone together without the kids to rekindle the spark that brought you together.

Family & Friends
Tip 26

**Date Night & Family Night**

Schedule It!
Life gets busy so you must put date night and family night on your monthly calendar.

Maybe you choose the first Saturday night of the month for date night. You can go out for a nice dinner or take a walk in a beautiful park. Be creative. You could even have a picnic on the floor in front of the fireplace in your living room. The main goal is to talk and connect.

Family night could be one Sunday evening a month. Family night is best if it is e-free. E-free means no electronics for a few hours. Put away the phones & tablets. Turn off the TV. Play a game or do a craft. Cook dinner together or bake a treat for the family. It is all about connection and creating memories.

Family & Friends
Tip 27

**Appreciate Who They Are**

When paying someone a compliment, don't just compliment what they do. Instead be sure to compliment the character of the person along with their attitude. For example, instead of "Thanks for making sure everything was set up for the family dinner." Say "Thank you for having a smile on your face and a pep in your step while getting everything set up for the family dinner."

Recognizing the attitude and character of someone raises your level of influence with that person. People want to be appreciated and encouraged. Take your compliments to the next level by focusing on character and attitude.

Family & Friends
Tip 28

**Family Meetings**

In order to have your family support your goals and dreams, they must feel a part of the entire process.

Schedule a family meeting so you can go over your goals and have everyone understand why you are willing to work so hard. Especially if you have children, they need to know what you are working on and why as a family you might have to make a few sacrifices.

Determine a reward for the entire family when a particular goal is accomplished. Having a reward that benefits every family member helps when you have to miss a baseball or soccer game. Every family member knows about the sacrifices that may be necessary to achieve the goal and the reward they will be part of when the goal is accomplished.

Family & Friends
Tip 29

**Family Treasure Map**

A treasure map or vision board (as they are popularly called)
is a collage of pictures of your dreams, goals and things that make you happy.

Spend some time with your family cutting out pictures from magazines of places you would like to vacation. Maybe it's a family cruise or a trip to Disneyworld. Do you want a lake house or a house in the mountains? Do you want a trampoline or a pool? Cut out pictures of things your family desires and glue them to a poster board.

Place the family treasure map where everyone can see it daily. It is a reminder of what the entire family is working towards. It will keep everyone motivated and moving forward in reaching the goals.

Family & Friends
Tip 30

### "Girl Time" "Guy Time"

Building friendships is critical to strong emotional health. How do you build relationships with your girl or guy friends? Quality time is the key. Get the guys together to play tennis, go hunting or camping, take a quick trip to Vegas or go fishing. Get the girls together for a spa day, a round of golf, a weekend at the lake house, coffee or a long walk in a beautiful park.

Having quality time helps you get to know a great deal about other people. What do they like? What do they dislike? I actually have an entire group of friends who are tomato haters! It bonds them and they make fun of those of us who enjoy tomatoes. Really!?!?! Yes, really. Time together is what brought about this fun connection and ribbing of each other.

Family & Friends
Tip 31

## Connection Events

Create a comfortable environment to connect in your home. Invite a couple of people or a large group. Make family & friends feel special by welcoming them into your home. Show them around. Give them permission to make themselves comfortable. Show them where the beverages are and make it clear they can help themselves at any time. Opening your home regularly helps others really see who you are on a day to day basis. Your home is a reflection of your values. People who come into your home that have similar values will feel a strong association to you.

When we have a dinner party in our home, we always have a question that everyone answers at dinner. We might ask "Where is your dream place to visit?" or "What is the best advice your parents gave you?"

Mentors
Tip 32

## Leaders are Readers

If you want to lead, you must be a reader! We have all heard the saying leaders are readers and readers are leaders. Reading improves our skills and thinking while making you a better person. Leaders are always learning and growing. If you go to any successful person's home you will find they have a library of great books. Success leaves clues. Just start reading 15 minutes a day and by the end of the year you will have read 15-20 great gooks. Here are just a few suggestions:

The Bible
Think & Grow Rich by Napoleon Hill
The Richest Man in Babylon by George Clason
Becoming a Person of Influence by John Maxwell
The Seasons of Life by Jim Rohn

Mentors
Tip 33

**Accountability Buddies**

An accountability buddy is someone that supports you in making sure you stay on track with you goals. Studies show that sharing your goal with another person increases the likelihood of you actually achieving your goal. Checking in with your accountability buddy can be as simple as a weekly scheduled phone call and a daily text confirming your actions towards your goal. Keep it simple. For a call, be sure to set a time limit. Share your success and your setbacks for the week. Discuss how you can make progress toward your goal in the coming week. Whatever your goal—weight loss, exercise, work promotion, connection to spouse—having an accountability buddy will aid in keeping you on track. Choose wisely. Find a positive person and set it up to be accountable to each other for your progress towards your goal.

Mentors
Tip 34

**Hire a Coach**

"We could all use a little coaching. When you're playing the game, it's hard to think of everything."
--Jim Rohn

Find a professional life, career or business coach. Have a weekly conversation about your goals, challenges and opportunities. A coach will push and prod you to raise your standards, teach you to ask for what you want, and help you shape your life and business to what you want it to be. Having a coach helps you get more of what you want (energy, time, money, etc.) and less of what you don't want (problems, confusion, stress, fatigue).

Hiring a coach doesn't have to be expensive. Ask business mentors you admire for referrals.

Mentors
Tip 35

**Board of Directors**

Companies have a Board of Directors to advise the upper level management on significant decisions. Create your own Board of Directors for your life and business. Admire the marriage of a friend? Meet them quarterly for half an hour and learn what makes their marriage so strong. Impressed by the results a friend is reaching in their sales career? Meet them quarterly and ask questions to learn how they prospect, follow-up and close. Respect the health and fitness of a co-worker? Connect with them quarterly to learn about their exercise routines, nutrition choices and any other ways they support being in excellent physical shape.

Commit to your willingness to implement the habits and behaviors you learn about from your board members.

Mentors
Tip 36

## Qualities of a Mentor

What are some of the qualities you want to look for in a mentor?

<u>Listening Skills</u>: Actively listening is an art that must be practiced. Listen respectfully with your full attention.

<u>Integrity</u>: Sound moral character and similar values.

<u>Successful</u>: Make sure your mentor has proven success in the area where you want to excel.

<u>Authentic</u>: Willingness to share skills, knowledge and expertise in a transparent manner.

<u>Positive</u>: Attitude is everything!

<u>Communication Skills</u>: Able to provide guidance and constructive feedback in a succinct, clear manner.

<u>Lifestyle</u>: Values others & motivates by setting a good example.

Mentors
Tip 37

**Pay It Forward**

"A mentor is someone who sees more talent and ability within you than you see in yourself and helps bring it out in you." --Bob Proctor

Be a mentor to others. Most people that have climbed the ladder of success had someone who believed in them before they fully believed in themselves. Being a mentor is about sharing your knowledge and experience with others. You are a mentor in so many roles—parent, teacher, coach, friend, business partner, supervisor, aunt or uncle. Consider how you weave mentoring into all areas of your life to help someone travel a journey you have already traveled and avoid some of the bumps along the way.

Referral Network
Tip 38

**Follow Your Money**

Who do you pay money to every month? When it comes to your business have the motto that you do business with people who do business with you. One way to build strong relationships within your referral network is to make sure your recommend the services of those in your sphere of influence whenever possible. If you have a product or service your purchase from someone, if they can do business with your product or service, they should reciprocate and be your customer. For example, if you are a residential remodeler and your insurance agent is going to remodel their home, they should at the very least request a quote from you and consider you for their remodel. You pay them for your insurance every year. They should be willing to do business with you. If not, it may be time to find a new insurance agent.

Referral Network
Tip 39

**Connecting in Groups**

It is important to build great relationships with your referral network. The key is to get involved. Join your local Chamber of Commerce, networking groups, meet-up groups, etc.

Your goal is to make a connection with a few key people on your way to expanding your network. Once you have identified an inner circle of contacts, respectfully ask those people to introduce you to their close contacts. Volunteer to help at meetings. Be an ambassador or a greeter. Even if it isn't in an official capacity, consider yourself as the welcome committee at events. Smile and shake hands with people as they arrive. If someone appears uncomfortable or not connecting to others, go over to them and start a conversation.

Ask questions. Don't talk about you. Ask about them.

Referral Network
Tip 40

**One on One Meetings**

Be interested!
A one on one meeting is set up to get to know about a person. We all prefer to do business with people we like and trust. Make sure you show genuine interest in the person you are investing time to meet. Find out about their family and what they love about their business. What are they passionate about?

Take the lead by asking them questions first. Ask how you can support them in their business. Generally this will lead to them asking you the same or similar questions. Answer authentically. Stay engaged. Take notes to show you are serious about building the relationship and what they are saying has value to you.

Referral Network
Tip 41

**Be Friendly!**

Want people to be drawn to you? SMILE! When meeting new people or reconnecting with acquaintances, be sure to look them in the eye and ask questions. Stephen Covey taught us to be more interested than interesting. Ask a question and actively listen to the answer while looking them in the eye. You don't have to stare them down. Just let them know you are completely present in the conversation and genuinely interested in their response.

Affirm their attendance at an event by saying "Glad you invested the time to join us today." or "Thanks for making time to be here today."

"A smile is the light in your window that tells others that there is a caring, sharing person inside." --Denis Waitley

Referral Network
Tip 42

**Connect on Social Media**

In today's digital world, one of the best ways to build rapport with your referral network is to connect with them on social media. After you meet someone at an event, be sure to get connected with them on LinkedIn, Google+, Facebook, Instagram, Pinterest, etc. If it feels appropriate when you connect with a new person, take a picture of the two of you to share on social media. You can even comment about the prospect of helping each other grow their business when you post the picture.

After you have connected, be sure to engage. Start or add to conversations. Recognize birthdays. Congratulate on their accomplishments. Applaud anniversaries. Celebrate with them when their favorite sports team wins. Stay connected.

Referral Network
Tip 43

**Follow Up!**

You may have heard the saying, "The fortune is in the follow up." It's absolutely true! It is vital in business and life to follow up with people.

What are the ideal ways to follow up? Maybe a quick phone call, a text or an email. If you double the time you follow up with people versus the time you spend networking, you will experience explosive growth in your business.

It is critical to schedule the time in your calendar for follow up. Otherwise, other activities get in the way and the time you invested networking to meet people was wasted because you never moved forward to begin establishing a long-term relationship with them.

Referral Network
Tip 44

**Know Their Name**

When we are born the name given to us becomes our identity. When our parents, siblings, friends or teacher want to get our attention, they call our name. When someone uses our name, it indicates they know us. It has been said that everyone's favorite word is their own name. When you use someone's name in a conversation, you are showing them how important they are to the communication. Using someone's name makes them feel incredibly valuable to the interaction.

How do you remember someone's name when you first meet them? Say their name back to them: "Nice to meet you, Jan." Now try to weave their name into the conversation 2-3 more times in the next few minutes. Now you will successfully remember their name the next time you meet.

Referral Network
Tip 45

## The Power of Influence

Influence is the ability to sway or alter an individual or group's thoughts, beliefs or actions. Being a person of influence is sharing your beliefs and values with others.

The power of influence can inspire and empower other men and women to go for their greatness. When you can make a difference in someone's life for the better, you have become influential. What is truly powerful is when the ripple effect takes place and they make the decision to go out and do the same for someone else.

"Think twice before you speak because your words and influence will plant the seed of either success or failure in the mind of another." – Napoleon Hill

### *A Note from Alice & Melynda*

Congratulations on your commitment to improve both your personal and business relationships.

Be sure to make a commitment to implement what you learned from these golden nuggets for building lifetime relationships.

We will continue to focus on deepening the relationships in our lives and purposefully meeting new people with which to grow relationships.

We challenge you to expand your sphere of influence. Remember to embrace people and make them feel important in your life. As your build your relationship skills, you will smoothly meet even more of your goals in life.

May your business thrive!

# About Alice Hinckley

Alice's passion is to help others grow their businesses and experience life more deeply via insightful coaching, informational presentations and high level life experiences.

Alice has been an entrepreneur for over twenty years. She has achieved President's Club status in both direct selling and corporate America. Alice continues to influence by speaking at personal development events to audiences of all sizes.

## Connect with Alice

www.yourlightbulbmoments.com
alice@yourlightbulbmoments.com

www.exploreambit.com

Facebook
www.facebook.com/lightbulbmoments
www.facebook.com/alice.hinckley
www.facebook.com/aliceambit

Twitter
www.twitter.com/alicehinckley

LinkedIn
www.linkedin.com/in/lightbulbmoments

# About Melynda Lilly

Melynda began her career in direct sales and network marketing over twenty-five years ago. She has built large organizations with the goal of helping average people earn an above average income so they can do things in life they are passionate about.

Melynda is incredibly passionate about her family which includes her husband of thirty-four years, Mark, three grown children and eight beautiful grandchildren.

**Connect with Melynda**

www.lilly.energygoldrush.com

mlilly@flash.net

Facebook
www.facebook.com/melyndalilly
www.facebook.com/ambitwithmelynda

Twitter
www.twitter.com/mklilly

# Other Books by Melynda & Alice

Behind Her Brand: Entrepreneur Edition Volume 1
(2015)
*Co-Author Melynda Lilly*

Women Entrepreneur Extraordinaire
(2013)
*Co-Author Alice L. Hinckley CPA*

Soar to Success When You Think Like a CEO
(2014)
*By Alice L. Hinckley CPA &
Elizabeth McCormick*

Behind Her Brand: Entrepreneur Edition Volume 4
(2015)
*Co-Author Alice Hinckley*

Behind Her Brand: Women of Influence
Equipping. Educating. Empowering
(2105)
*Compiled by Melynda Lilly & Alice Hinckley*

Nail it in 90!
For Direct Selling & Network Marketing
Professionals
By Kim Johnson & Alice Hinckley

www.ingramcontent.com/pod-product-compliance
Lightning Source LLC
Chambersburg PA
CBHW050023230526
45470CB00003B/1095